W9-ASB-848

# CONTENTS

# 🌿 Lake Classic Short Stories 🌿

*"The universe is made of stories, not atoms."*

—Muriel Rukeyser

*"The story's about you."*

—Horace

Everyone loves a good story. It is hard to think of a friendlier introduction to classic literature. For one thing, short stories are *short*—quick to get into and easy to finish. Of all the literary forms, the short story is the least intimidating and the most approachable.

Great literature is an important part of our human heritage. In the belief that this heritage belongs to everyone, *Lake Classic Short Stories* are adapted for today's readers. Lengthy sentences and paragraphs are shortened. Archaic words are replaced. Modern punctuation and spellings are used. Many of the longer stories are abridged. In all the stories,

5

painstaking care has been taken to preserve the author's unique voice.

*Lake Classic Short Stories* have something for everyone. The hundreds of stories in the collection cover a broad terrain of themes, story types, and styles. Literary merit was a deciding factor in story selection. But no story was included unless it was as enjoyable as it was instructive. And special priority was given to stories that shine light on the human condition.

Each book in the *Lake Classic Short Stories* is devoted to the work of a single author. Little-known stories of merit are included with famous old favorites. Taken as a whole, the collected authors and stories make up a rich and diverse sampler of the story-teller's art.

*Lake Classic Short Stories* guarantee a great reading experience. Readers who look for common interests, concerns, and experiences are sure to find them. Readers who bring their own gifts of perception and appreciation to the stories will be doubly rewarded.

# ❧ Sherwood Anderson ❧
## (1876–1941)

## About the Author

Sherwood Anderson grew up in the small town of Clyde, Ohio. His sometimes-employed father was a sign painter who had trouble supporting his family. The third of seven children, Anderson had boyhood jobs as a paperboy and racetrack stableboy. Because he had to help support his family, he dropped out of high school before completing his first year.

At age 20, Anderson left Clyde and moved to Chicago. There he worked as a stock handler in a warehouse and then as a writer of advertising copy. After meeting such Chicago writers as Carl Sandburg and Theodore Dreiser, he started his own literary career. In 1907, he bought and then ran a paint factory, while writing at night. In 1912, he suffered a mental collapse—probably because he had been working too hard. When he recovered, he looked upon his breakdown as a turning point and a "rebirth." After that he decided "to be a servant to words alone."

From then on, Anderson was a full-time writer. His most important novel, *Winesburg, Ohio*, is sometimes seen as a revolt against small-town life. But others see it as a celebration of the "little people" who are everyone's neighbors, sisters, brothers, and friends. When this novel was published in 1919, Anderson became very popular among the young people in America.

The underlying theme of Anderson's writing is the loneliness of the individual. He saw mature relationships between men and woman as one way—probably the best way—to find happiness.

If you enjoy stories about the sights and sounds of common, everyday life, you'll enjoy reading Sherwood Anderson.

# Sophistication

Moving from one stage of life to another can be unsettling and frightening. In this tender story, a young man and woman reach the same turning point at the same time. Read on to discover how an old friendship can inspire new courage.

ALL ALONG HE HAD NOTICED HER GROWING INTO A
WOMAN AS HE GREW INTO A MAN.

# Sophistication

It was early evening of a day in the late fall. The Winesburg County Fair had brought crowds of country people into town. The day had been clear, and the night came on warm and pleasant. The road that stretched between the berry fields was now covered with dry brown leaves. The dust from passing wagons rose up in clouds.

Children, curled into little balls, slept on straw-covered wagon beds. Their hair was full of dust, and their fingers were black and sticky. As the dust rolled over the fields, the setting sun turned it bright with color.

In the main street of the town, crowds filled the stores and sidewalks. Night came on, horses whinnied, and the clerks in stores ran madly about. Lost children cried for their mothers. An American town works hard even at the task of amusing itself.

Young George Willard had pushed his way through the crowds on Main Street. Now he hid himself under a stairway and stood looking at the people. With bright eyes, he watched the figures passing under the store lights. Thoughts kept coming into his head—and he did not want to think. He tapped his foot on the wooden steps and looked sharply about. "Well, is she going to stay with him all day? Have I done all this waiting for nothing?" he said under his breath.

George Willard, the Ohio village boy, was fast becoming a man. New thoughts kept coming into his mind. All that day, amid the crowd of people at the fair, he had gone about feeling lonely. Soon he would leave Winesburg. In some faraway city, he hoped to get work on a news-paper. Just the idea of it made him feel grown up.

This mood that had come over him was a thing known to men rather than boys. For some reason it made him feel old and a little tired. Memories awoke in him. In his mind, this new sense of being grown-up set him apart from others. It made him sad. The first time he had felt this way was just after his mother's death. Now he wanted to understand the feeling.

There is a moment when every boy has this feeling for the first time. Suddenly he looks back on his life instead of forward. Perhaps this is when he crosses the line into manhood.

It might happen on a day like any other. The boy is walking through the streets of his town. He is thinking of the future and all that he will do in the world. Then suddenly something happens. He stops under a tree and waits—as if to hear a voice that is calling his name. Ghosts of old things creep into his mind. Voices outside of himself whisper that perhaps he is expecting too much from this life. Something in him changes. From being quite sure of himself and his future, he becomes not at all sure.

Those boys who look deeply at life might suddenly see the faces of men who have lived before them. They realize that these men of the past came out of nothingness into the world. They lived their lives and again disappeared into nothingness. Suddenly, the boy is wiser to the ways of life. It is the sadness of sophistication that has come to him.

With a little gasp, he sees himself as no more than a leaf blown along by the wind. He knows that he must live and die without ever being sure of tomorrow. He gives a little shiver. He looks eagerly about. The 18 years that he has already lived seem to have been only a moment. Already he hears death calling.

At such a time a boy wants to come close to some other human. With all his heart, he longs to touch someone. And he wants to be touched by the hand of another. Often he would like that other to be a woman, because he believes a woman will be gentle. She will understand. That's want he wants most of all—understanding.

When the moment of sophistication came to George Willard, his mind turned to Helen White. Helen was the daughter of the town banker. All along he had noticed her growing into a woman as he grew into a man. He remembered a sweet summer night when he was 18. As he was walking with her on a country road, he had boasted, hoping to look important in her eyes.

Tonight he wanted to see her for another reason. He wanted to tell her about the new thoughts that had come to him. Once, when he knew nothing, he had tried to make her think of him as a man. Now he wanted her to see the change that had taken place in him.

As for Helen White, she also had come to a time of change. What George felt, she—in her young woman's way—felt also. She was no longer a girl. Now she longed for the grace and beauty that belonged to a woman. Helen was going to college in Cleveland. She had come home to spend a day at the fair. Like George, she too had begun to have memories.

During her day at the fair, Helen sat in the grandstand with a young man. He was one of the teachers from the college and a guest of her mother's. The young man's manner was very wise and worldly. In truth, however, he was rather bossy and boring. Helen felt at once that he would not do for her purpose. But she was glad to be seen in his company at the fair. He was well dressed, and he was a stranger. She knew that everyone would notice them, and that thought made her happy.

While they sat together that afternoon, she paid so much attention to the teacher that he grew interested. Helen was beginning to seem like the perfect girl for him. "A teacher needs money," he thought. "I should marry a woman with money." But when night came on, Helen began to grow restless. She wanted to send the teacher away.

Helen White was thinking of George Willard at the same time that he was thinking of her. She remembered the summer evening when they had walked together. She wanted to walk with him again. Helen had spent months in the city. She had gone to theaters and been part of the great crowds in the bright streets. These things, she thought, had changed her. Now she wanted George to feel and understand the change in her nature.

The memory of their last summer evening together was fresh in both of their minds. But in fact that evening had been spent rather stupidly. They had walked out of town along a country road. Then they had stopped by a fence near a field of young corn. George had taken off his coat and let it hang on his arm.

"Well, I've stayed here in Winesburg,

yes. I've not gone away yet, but I'm growing up," he had said. "I've been reading books and thinking. I'm going to try to amount to something in life."

Then he stopped and thought about his own words. "Well," he tried to explain, "that isn't the point, I suppose. Perhaps I'd better quit talking."

The confused boy put his hand on the girl's arm. His voice shook. The two started to walk back toward town. Feeling he must say something, George started to brag. "Someday I'm going to be a big man—the biggest that ever lived here in Winesburg," he declared. "I want you to do something, Helen. Perhaps it's none of my business. But I want you to try to be different from other women. You see the point. It's none of my business. But I want you to be a beautiful woman. You see what I want."

The boy's voice trailed off. In silence the two came back into town and went along the street to Helen's house. At the gate he tried again to say something important. Speeches he had practiced came into his head, but they seemed all wrong now. "I thought—I used to think—I had it in my mind that you would marry Seth Richmond. Now I know you won't." That was all he could find to say before she went through the gate and into her house.

Now, on this warm fall evening, George stood under the stairway, watching the crowd on Main Street. He thought of his talk with Helen beside the cornfield. He was ashamed of the way he must have sounded. He looked back into the street. Hundreds of people moved up and down like cattle in a pen. Buggies and wagons almost filled the narrow road. Young boys with shining red faces walked about with girls on their arms. A band began to play in a room above one of the stores. The sound of music floated down through an open window and out across the hum of voices.

All the noises got on young George's nerves. Everywhere, on all sides, the sense of crowding, moving life closed in on him. He wanted to run away by himself and think.

"If she wants to stay with that fellow, she can just do it. Why should I care? What difference does it make to me?" he growled to himself. He went along Main Street and turned into a side street.

George felt so completely lonely and sad that he wanted to cry. But his pride made him walk quickly along, swinging his arms. He came to Westley Moyer's stable. There he stopped to listen to some men. They were talking about a race that Westley's horse had won at the fair that afternoon. Westley was walking up and down, boasting to the small crowd. He held a whip in his hand and kept tapping it on the ground. Little puffs of dust rose in the lamplight.

"I wasn't afraid for a minute," Westley exclaimed. "I knew I had them beat all the time. I wasn't afraid."

On any other day, George Willard would have been interested in Westley's boasting. Now it made him angry. He turned away and hurried down the street. "Old fool," he said under his breath. "Why does he want to be bragging? Why doesn't he just shut up?"

As he cut through an empty lot, George tripped over a pile of garbage. A nail from an empty barrel tore his pants. Now he lost his temper completely. He sat down on the ground and swore. Then he fixed the torn place with a pin, got up, and went on. "I'll go to Helen White's house, that's what I'll do. I'll walk right in. I'll say that I want to see her. I'll walk right in and sit down. That's what I'll do," he declared. He climbed over a fence and began to run.

On the front porch of her house, Helen White was finding it hard to sit still. The teacher sat between Helen and her mother. His talk about life in the city bored the girl. He was trying so hard to seem worldly! For the moment he seemed to have forgotten that he had grown up in a small Ohio town. "Thank you for inviting me, Mrs. White," he was saying. "You have given me a chance to study the type of small town from which most of our students come. It was very good of you to have me down for the day." Then he turned to Helen and smiled. "Your life is still wrapped up with the life of this town?" he asked. "There are people here in whom you are interested?" To the girl his voice sounded stuffy and proud.

Helen got up. She went into the house. At the door leading to the garden, she stood listening for a moment. Her mother began to talk. "There is no one here fit to keep company with a girl of Helen's fine breeding," Mrs. White said.

Helen ran down the stairs at the back of the house. She stopped in the garden and stood shaking in the dark. It seemed to her that the whole world was full of foolish people saying foolish words. She ran through the garden gate and into a little side street. "George! Where are you, George?" she cried. Suddenly she was filled with excitement. She stopped running then and leaned against a tree. Without quite knowing why, she began to laugh wildly.

Along the dark little street came George Willard. He was still talking out loud to himself. "I'm going to walk straight into her house. I'll go right in and sit down," he was saying as he came up to her. Then he stopped and stared stupidly. "Come on," he said, taking hold of her hand. With hanging heads, the two young people walked along the street under the trees. Dry leaves rustled under foot. He had found her. Now George wondered what he should do and say.

At one end of the Winesburg fair ground, there is an old grandstand. It has never been painted, and the boards are rotted and worn. The fair ground stands on top of a low hill. From the grandstand, the lights of the town sparkle against the night sky.

George and Helen climbed the hill to the fair ground. The loneliness George had felt in the crowded streets was both broken and made stronger by Helen's company. And Helen was having the same feelings.

There are always two forces fighting in young people. The warm, unthinking little animal inside struggles against the other force that thinks, reasons, and remembers. It was that second, more sophisticated force that was winning out in George Willard. Helen sensed his mood. When they got to the grandstand, they climbed under the roof. In a moment they were sitting down on one of the long benches.

There is something amazing about a midwestern fair ground on the night the fair closes. The emptiness sparks a feeling that is never to be forgotten. On all sides are ghosts—not of the dead, but of living people. Here, during the day just passed, people have poured in from the town and the country. Farmers with their wives and children have gathered here. Young girls have laughed, and men with beards have talked about their lives. The place has been filled to overflowing with life. And now that it is night, all that life has all gone away. The silence is almost terrifying.

On the one hand, there is the frightening thought that life has little meaning. Yet, on the other hand, the people of the town now seem very close and dear. The love of life is then so deep that tears come into the eyes.

In the darkness under the roof of the grandstand, George Willard sat close beside Helen White. He felt how very small he was compared to the whole huge world. All the people in town, so busy with their daily lives, had made him feel weary. Now, that weariness was gone. Being with Helen made him feel new and fresh again. It was as though her gentle woman's hand was helping him fix what was wrong with his life.

Now he began to think about the people in the town where he had always lived. He felt something like new love and respect for them—and for Helen, too. He wanted to love and be loved by her. But he did not, at that moment, want to be confused by romance. In the dark, he took hold of her hand. When she moved closer, he put his arm around her shoulder. A soft wind began to blow.

With all his might, he tried to understand the mood that had come upon him. In that high place in the darkness, the two held each other and waited. In the mind of each was the same thought: "I have come to this lonely place and here is this other."

In Winesburg, the crowded day had turned into the long night of late fall. Farm horses tramped down lonely country roads, pulling their loads of sleepy people. Clerks began to lock the doors of stores. In the Opera House, a crowd had gathered to see a show. Farther down Main Street the band played, keeping the feet of the young flying over a dance floor.

But in the darkness of the grandstand, Helen White and George Willard were silent. Now and then the spell that held them was broken. Then they turned and tried to see into each other's eyes in the dim light. They kissed, but only briefly. At the upper end of the fair ground, they could see some men working with horses that had raced that afternoon. The men had built a fire. When the wind blew, little flames danced crazily about.

At last George and Helen got up from their bench. They walked away into the darkness. Soon they came to a path that led past a field of corn that had not yet been cut. The wind whispered among the dry corn stalks. Farther on, they stopped by a tree. George again put his hands on the girl's shoulders. She hugged him eagerly. But then, once more they drew quickly away from each other.

Romance was cooled by their mood. They stopped kissing and stood a little apart. They were both embarrassed. To end their embarrassment, they began to play as children do, laughing and wrestling with each other. They became not man and woman, not boy and girl, but excited little animals.

And so they went down the hill. In the darkness they were two fine young things, playing in a young world. Once, running forward, Helen tripped George. He fell, shaking with laughter, and rolled down the hill. Helen ran after him, and then for just a moment, she stopped in the darkness.

There is no way of knowing what woman's thoughts went through her mind. But at the bottom of the hill she came up to the boy. She took his arm and walked beside him in friendly silence.

For some reason that neither one of them could have explained, their evening together had given them just what they needed. Man or boy, woman or girl, they had for one moment taken hold of something priceless. It is the thing that makes the life of men and women in the modern world possible.

# The Untold Lie

Have you ever heard of a "magic moment" in someone's life? For Ray Pearson, that moment came on a golden autumn afternoon. In a flash he saw a "truth" that he had never seen before. Would he be able to warn his friend in time? *Should* he?

"Has a fellow got to be harnessed up and driven through life like a horse?"

# The Untold Lie

Ray Pearson and Hal Winters were farm hands. They worked on a farm three miles north of Winesburg. On Saturday afternoons they came into town to wander about the streets with other fellows from the country.

Ray was a quiet, rather nervous man. He was about 50 years old and had a lined face and shoulders rounded by too much hard work. In his nature he was as unlike Hal Winters as two men can be unlike.

Ray was an altogether serious man. He had a little wife with a sharp, pointy nose and a sharp voice. The two of them had six skinny children. They lived in a tumble-down frame house. The place was beside a creek at the back end of the Wills farm where Ray worked.

Hal Winters, who worked on the Wills farm too, was a younger fellow. Hal was the third son of an old man called Windpeter Winters. Windpeter had a sawmill near Unionville, six miles away. He was looked upon by everyone in Winesburg as a low-down, tricky fellow.

People from that part of Ohio will remember old Windpeter for his strange and sad death. It happened when he came into town one night and had too much to drink. He started to drive home to Unionville along the train tracks. The town butcher, who happened to live out that way, stopped Windpeter at the edge of town. He warned him that the train might hit him head on if he kept to the tracks. But Windpeter slashed at him with his buggy whip and drove on. The train struck and killed him and his two horses.

A farmer and his wife saw the accident. They said that old Windpeter stood up on the seat of his wagon and shouted at the oncoming engine. They said he had maddened his horses by slashing at them. They heard him scream with delight as the horses rushed ahead to certain death.

Everyone in our town said the old man would go straight to the devil. They said the town would be better off without him. But boys like young George Willard and Seth Richmond had a different idea. They thought secretly that old Windpeter knew what he was doing. In a strange way, they even admired his foolish courage. Like most boys, they sometimes wished that they might die in glory someday. Just being grocery clerks and going about their everyday lives didn't seem very important.

But this is not the story of Windpeter Winters. And it is not yet the story of his son Hal—the man who worked on the Wills farm with Ray Pearson. It is Ray's story. It is only necessary to talk of young

Hal so that you will be able to get into the spirit of the story.

Hal was a bad one. Everyone said that. There were three boys in the Winters family—John, Hal, and Edward. All were big fellows, like old Windpeter himself. And all were fighters and woman-chasers and all-around bad ones.

Hal was the worst of the lot. He was always up to something. Once he stole a load of boards from his father's mill and sold them in Winesburg. With that money he had bought himself a suit of flashy clothes. His father had come charging into town to find him. When they met, they fought with their fists on Main Street. Both men were arrested and put into jail.

Hal worked on the Wills farm for a special reason. There was a country school teacher out that way who had caught his eye. He was only 22 at the time. But he had already had what the people in town called 'women problems.' Everyone who knew of his interest in the school teacher was sure that it would turn out badly in the end.

On a day in late October, Ray and Hal were at work in a field. They were husking corn. Once in a while something was said and they laughed. But most of the time there was silence. Ray had dry, wind-burned hands that were bothering him. For a moment he put them into his pockets and looked away across the fields. He was in a sad, thoughtful mood that was made sadder by the beauty of the country. If you knew the Winesburg country in the fall, you could picture the low hills all splashed with yellows and reds. You would understand his feeling.

Ray began to think of a time long ago. He was a young fellow then, living with his father, a Winesburg baker. On fall days such as this, he had often wandered away to the woods. There he would gather nuts, hunt rabbits, or just hang around. His marriage had come about through one of his days of wandering. He had asked a girl who worked at his father's shop to go along with him—and something had happened.

Standing there in the corn field, he was thinking of that afternoon and how it had changed his whole life. Suddenly he felt angry. He had forgotten about Hal and found himself talking out loud. *"Tricked,* by gosh, that's what I was. I was tricked by life and made a fool of," he said in a low voice.

As though understanding his thoughts, Hal Winters spoke up. "Well, has it been worthwhile? What about it? What about marriage and all that?" he asked. Then he laughed. Hal tried to keep on laughing, but he, too, was in a serious mood. He began to talk quietly. "Has a fellow *got* to do it?" he asked. "Has he got to be harnessed up and driven through life like a horse?"

Hal didn't wait for an answer. He jumped to his feet and began to walk back and forth between the corn rows. Something was making him more and more excited. Bending down suddenly, he picked up an ear of the yellow corn. He threw it at the fence. "Nell Gunther's going to have a baby," he said in a rush. "I'm telling you—but you keep your mouth shut."

Ray Pearson stood up and stared. He was almost a foot shorter than Hal. Hal put his two hands on the older man's shoulders. They made quite a picture, standing in the big empty field. The quiet cornstalks framed them from behind, and the red and yellow hills glowed in the distance. No longer were they just two men working the same job. Now they had become something real and alive to each other. Hal sensed it, and then he laughed.

"Well, old daddy," he said a bit stiffly, "come on, *help* me. I've got Nell in trouble. Maybe you've been in the same fix yourself. I know what everyone would say is the right thing to do—but what do *you* say? Shall I marry and settle down? Shall I put myself into the harness to be worn out like an old horse? Shall I do that? Or shall I tell Nell to go to the devil? Come on—you tell me. Whatever you say, Ray, I'll do."

Ray couldn't answer. He shook Hal's hands loose. Then he turned and walked straight away toward the barn. He was a man who felt things deeply, and there were tears in his eyes. He knew there was only one thing to say to Hal Winters, son of old Windpeter. There was only one thing that all his own training could bring him to say. There was only one thing that people would say was right. But for his life he couldn't say what he knew he should say.

At half-past four that afternoon, Ray was working in the barnyard. His wife came up the lane along the creek. She called to him. After the talk with Hal, he hadn't returned to the cornfield but worked about the barn. He had seen Hal come out of the farmhouse and go into the road. It looked like Hal was dressed up and ready for a night in town.

Now Ray followed his wife along the path to his own house. He looked at the

ground as he walked. He couldn't figure
out what was wrong. Every time he
raised his eyes and saw the beauty of
the country, he felt unsettled. He wanted
to do something he had never done before. He wanted to scream out, or shake
his wife, or something else just as
surprising and frightening. Along the
path he went, scratching his head and
trying to figure it out. He looked hard at
his wife's back, but she seemed the same
as she always had.

She only wanted him to go into town
for food. Then as soon as she had told
him what she wanted, she began to scold.
"You're always wasting time," she said.
"Now I want you to be quick. There isn't
anything in the house for supper. You've
got to get to town and back in a hurry."

Ray went into his house and took his
coat from a hook behind the door. It was
torn about the pockets. The collar was
worn. His wife went into the bedroom.
She came out with a cloth bag in one
hand and three silver dollars in the
other. Somewhere in the house a child

cried. A dog that had been sleeping by the stove sat up and yawned. Again the wife scolded. "The children will cry and cry until they get their supper. Why are you always so slow?"

Ray went out of the house and started off across a field. It was just growing dark. The land that lay before him was beautiful. All the low hills were washed with color. To Ray Pearson, the whole world seemed to have come alive in a magical way. Somehow it was just like that moment when he and Hal stood in the cornfield, staring into each other's eyes. The two men had come alive then.

The fall beauty of the Winesburg countryside was too much for Ray on that evening. That is all there was to it. He could not stand it. All of a sudden he forgot that he was a quiet old farm hand. Throwing off the torn coat, he began to run across the field. As he ran, he shouted out against his lost chances, against all the disappointments of life. He cried out against everything that makes life ugly.

"There was no promise made!" he cried into the empty spaces. "I didn't promise my Minnie anything. Hal hasn't made any promise to Nell. I know he hasn't. She went into the woods with him because she wanted to go. Why should I pay? Why should Hal pay? Why should anyone pay? I don't want Hal to become old and worn out. I'll tell him. I won't let it go on. I'll catch Hal before he gets to town, and I'll tell him."

Ray ran ahead without looking where he was going. Once he fell down. "I must catch Hal and tell him," he kept on thinking. Soon his breath came in gasps, but he kept running harder. As he ran, he remembered things that hadn't come into his mind for years. He thought about the years before he had married. He had planned to go out West then. He hadn't wanted to be a farm hand. He thought that when he got out West, he might go to sea and be a sailor. Or maybe he would get a job on a ranch and ride a horse into Western towns. There he would shout and laugh and wake the people in the houses with his wild cries. Then, as he ran, he remembered his children. He imagined that he felt their hands pulling at him. It seemed the children were pulling at Hal, too.

Darkness began to spread over the fields as Ray Pearson ran on. Now his breath came in little sobs. When he reached the fence at the edge of the road, he met Hal Winters. The young man was all dressed up, walking along with a quick step. Suddenly Ray did not have the words to say what he was thinking.

Ray Pearson lost his nerve. This fact is really the end of his story. It was almost dark when he got to the fence. He put his hands on the top bar and stood staring. Hal Winters jumped over a ditch and came up close to him. He put his hands into his pockets and laughed. Hal seemed to have lost his own sense of what had happened in the cornfield. Then he reached out a strong hand and took hold of Ray's shirt. He shook the old man as he might have shaken a bad dog.

"You came to tell me, huh?" he said. "Well, never mind telling me anything. I'm not afraid. I've already made up my mind." He laughed again and jumped back across the ditch. "Nell ain't no fool," he said. "She didn't ask me to marry her. I *want* to marry her. I want to settle down and have kids."

Ray Pearson also laughed. Suddenly he felt like laughing at himself and all the world.

Hal Winters moved off, fading into the darkness on the road that led to Winesburg. Ray turned and walked slowly back across the fields. He went to the place where he had left his torn coat. Some thought of a pleasant evening spent with his thin-legged children must have come into his mind. Or maybe he was thinking of a hot supper in his tumble-down house by the creek. Then he muttered to himself. "It's just as well. Whatever I told him would have just been a lie," he said softly. Then he also disappeared into the dark fields.

# Paper Pills

An ordinary man may have more drama in his life than anyone guesses. In this close-up picture of a small town doctor, the author gives us clues about the inner joys and sorrows of a misunderstood man.

ON SCRAPS OF PAPER, HE WROTE DOWN THOUGHTS—
THE ENDS OF THOUGHTS AND THE BEGINNINGS OF
THOUGHTS.

# Paper Pills

He was an old man with a white beard and a huge nose and hands. Long ago, he had been a doctor. In those days he drove a tired white horse from house to house through the streets of Winesburg. Later he married a girl who had money. When her father died, she had been left a large rich farm. The girl was quiet, tall, and dark. To many people she seemed very beautiful. Everyone in Winesburg wondered why she married the doctor. Within a year after the marriage, she died.

The knuckles of the doctor's hands were surprisingly large. When his hands were closed, those knuckles looked like unpainted wooden balls as large as walnuts. The doctor smoked a pipe. After his wife's death he sat all day in his empty office. His chair was next to a window that was covered with cobwebs. Once, on a hot day in August, he had tried to open the window—but he found that it was stuck fast. After that he forgot all about it.

Winesburg had forgotten the old man. But in Doctor Reefy there were the seeds of something very fine. Alone in his stuffy office above the dry goods store, he worked constantly. His work was to build up little piles of truths. Then he would knock them down again, only to build other piles.

Doctor Reefy was a tall man who had worn one suit of clothes for ten years. Now his suit was thin at the sleeves and had little holes at the knees and elbows. In the office he wore a loose jacket with huge pockets over his suit. Into those pockets he constantly stuffed scraps of paper. After some weeks those scraps of paper turned into hard little balls. When his pockets would hold no more, he dumped them out upon the floor.

For ten years Dr. Reefy had but one friend, another old man named John Spaniard. Spaniard owned a tree farm. Sometimes, in a playful mood, old Doctor Reefy threw a handful of the paper balls at the tree man. "This should confuse you!" the doctor would say. "You think the world is so fine a place!" Then the doctor would shake with laughter.

The story of Doctor Reefy is a very curious one. It has to do with the tall dark girl who became his wife and left her money to him. It is a delicious story, like the twisted little apples that grow on the trees of Winesburg. If you walk among the trees in the fall, the ground is hard with frost. The biggest apples have been picked. They have been put in barrels and shipped to cities. There they will be eaten in apartments that are filled with books, magazines, furniture, and people.

On the trees, only a few bumpy little apples are left. These are the ones that the pickers have passed over. They look like the knuckles of Doctor Reefy's hands. But when you bite into them, they are delicious. There is a little round sweet place at the side of these apples. People who understand this run from tree to tree over the frosted ground picking the bumpy, twisted apples. They fill their pockets with them. But only the few know the sweetness of the twisted apples.

The girl and Doctor Reefy began meeting on a summer afternoon. He was only 45 then. Already he had begun filling his pockets with scraps of paper that were to become hard balls. He had formed this odd habit as he sat in his buggy behind the slow-moving old white horse. He began making the balls as he went slowly along country roads. On the scraps of paper, he wrote down thoughts—the ends of thoughts, and the beginnings of thoughts.

One by one Doctor Reefy's thoughts had added up. After a while they would form a gigantic truth. But as the truth formed in his mind, it clouded the world. It became terrible. Then it faded away, and the little thoughts began again.

The tall dark girl came to see Doctor Reefy because she was going to have a baby. She was frightened.

Her father and mother had died, leaving her their rich farm lands. This set a train of men on her heels. Each hoped to marry the girl and take over her property. For two years she saw a man almost every evening. Except for two, her suitors were all alike. They talked to her of love. They sounded eager when they spoke to her, but there was a greedy look in their eyes.

The two men who were different were not like each other at all. One was a thin young man with white hands. He was the son of a jeweler in Winesburg. He was a very serious fellow who liked to talk to her about goodness and purity. The other, a black-haired boy with large ears, had little to say. But he always managed to get her into the darkness, where he started to kiss her.

For a time the tall dark girl thought she would marry the jeweler's son. For hours she sat in silence, listening as he talked to her. But something about him frightened her. Beneath all his talk of goodness, she sensed something bad. At times it seemed to her that as he talked, he was holding her body in his hands. She imagined him turning her slowly about in his white hands and staring at her. At night she dreamed that the jeweler's son had bitten into her and that his jaws were dripping. She had the dream three times. Then she went off with the black-haired boy. He said nothing at all, but once he actually did bite her shoulder. The marks of his teeth showed for days.

After the girl came to know Doctor Reefy, she decided that she never wanted to leave him again. She knew he was a special man when she went into his office that morning. Without her saying anything, he seemed to know what had happened to her.

Another woman was in the office of the doctor that day. She was the wife of the man who owned the Winesburg book store. Like all old-fashioned country doctors, Doctor Reefy also pulled teeth. The woman was there to have her tooth pulled. Her husband was with her. When the tooth came out, they both screamed and blood ran down on the woman's white dress. The tall dark girl did not pay much attention. When the woman and the man had gone, the doctor smiled. "I will take you driving into the country with me," he said.

For several weeks the tall dark girl and the doctor were together almost every day. Then she became ill, and her baby died before it was born. But she was happy with the doctor. She was like one who has discovered the sweetness of the twisted apples. She could not ever think again of the round, perfect fruit that is eaten in city apartments.

In the fall that followed her first meeting with Doctor Reefy, she married him. In the next spring, she died. During the winter, he read to her all the odds and ends of thoughts he had written on the bits of paper. After he had read them, he laughed. Then he stuffed them away in his pockets to become round hard balls.

# An Awakening

Can a bad experience ever be a good teacher? In this touching story, young George Willard learns a lesson he won't soon forget. But who wanted to find out how quickly a romantic fantasy can turn into a nightmare?

WHEN SHE CAME TO THE DOOR HE LOST HIS NERVE.
AND THAT MADE HIM ANGRY.

# An Awakening

Belle Carpenter had dark skin, gray eyes, and thick lips. She was tall and strong. When bad thoughts came to her, she grew angry. Then she wished she were a man so she could fight someone with her fists. She worked in a hat shop. During the day she sat trimming hats by a window at the rear of the store.

Belle was the daughter of Henry Carpenter, the bookkeeper at the First National Bank of Winesburg. She lived with him in a gloomy old house at the end of a street. The house was circled by pine trees, and there was no grass beneath the trees. A broken gutter was loose at the back of the roof. When the wind blew, that gutter made a sad drumming noise. Sometimes the drumming sound went on all through the night.

Henry Carpenter had made life terrible for Belle when she was a young girl. But as she grew up, he lost his power over her. The bookkeeper was a picky man who wanted everything to be exactly so.

When he went to the bank in the morning, he put on an old black wool coat. When he returned home at night, he put on another black wool coat. Every evening he pressed the clothes he had worn in the streets. He had made special boards for this pressing. Each morning he wiped the boards with a wet cloth. Then he stood them upright behind the dining room door. If they were moved during the day, he became so angry that he could hardly speak.

Actually, the bookkeeper was afraid of his daughter. He realized that she was the only one who knew how badly he had treated her mother. She hated him for it. One day she went home at noon and carried a handful of soft mud into the house. With the mud, she rubbed the boards her father used for pressing his suits. Then she went back to her work feeling quite happy.

Sometimes Belle Carpenter walked out in the evening with George Willard. Secretly, she loved another man—but this love caused her much worry. She was in love with Ed Handby, a bartender in Ed Griffith's Saloon. The only reason she went about with the young reporter, George, was to hide her feelings. She believed that her station in life was much higher than the bartender's. So she walked about under the trees with George Willard. She let him kiss her. She felt that she could keep the younger man within bounds. About Ed Handby, she was not so sure.

Handby, the bartender, was a tall, broad-shouldered man of 30. He lived in a room above Griffith's saloon. His fists were large and his eyes small. But his voice, as though trying to hide the power of his fists, was soft and quiet. Still, there were stories told about him. Some people said they had seen the bartender going wild, getting in fights, smashing windows, and breaking chairs.

On the surface, the romance between Ed Handby and Belle Carpenter came to nothing. He had actually spent but one evening in her company. On that evening he hired a horse and buggy and took her for a drive. He decided then that she was the woman he needed and wanted. The bartender was ready to marry. He had already begun to save money for his wife. But he found it hard to explain his feelings in words. That night he took Belle into his arms and held her tightly. Then he brought her back to town and let her out of the buggy. "When I get hold of you again, I'll not let you go," he said as he turned to drive away. "You might as well make up your mind to that. It's you and me."

One night in January, George Willard went for a walk under a new moon. In Ed Handby's mind, George Willard was the only thing standing between him and Belle Carpenter. Early that evening, George had gone to the pool room. The place was filled with Winesburg boys, talking of women. The young reporter had talked too. He had said that women should look out for themselves. He said that the fellow who went out with a girl was not responsible for what happened. Then all the boys had told stories and boasted.

Later, George Willard went out of the pool room and into Main Street. For days the weather had been bitter cold. A high wind had blown down on the town from Lake Erie, some 18 miles to the north. But on that night the wind had died away. A new moon was shining. Without thinking where he was going or what he wanted to do, George turned off of Main Street. He began walking in the dimly lit streets that were lined by frame houses.

Because it was dark and he was alone, George began to talk aloud. He was in a playful mood and he tripped along the street, pretending to be drunk. Then he imagined that he was a soldier. He pictured himself wearing boots that reached to his knees and a sword that jingled as he walked. He imagined that he was an officer, passing before a long line of men who stood at attention. "Your uniform is not in order!" he yelled at an imaginary soldier. "How many times will I have to speak of this matter? Everything must be in order here. We have a hard job before us, and no hard job can be done without order."

He liked the sound of his own words, and continued on. "In every little thing, there must be order. I myself must be orderly. I must learn the law. I must get myself in touch with something orderly and big that swings through the night like a star. In my little way, I must begin to learn something—to work with life and with the law."

George Willard stopped by a fence near a street lamp. He began to shake. He had never before had such thoughts. Now he wondered where these ideas had come from. It seemed to him that some voice outside of himself had been talking as he walked along. "To come out of the pool room and think things like that," he whispered. "If I talked like that to the boys, they would never understand. I'm glad that they will never know what I've been thinking down here."

In Winesburg, as in all Ohio towns of that time, there was a section where the day laborers lived. The time of factories had not yet come. These workers found jobs in the fields or were hands on the railroads. They worked 12 full hours a day and received one dollar for the long day of work. These laborers lived in small, cheaply built houses with gardens in the back. A few of them kept cows and perhaps a pig in a little shed at the rear of the garden.

George Willard walked into such a street on this clear January night. His head was full of important thoughts. The street was dimly lighted. In some places there was no sidewalk at all. He was already feeling excited, but now something about the place excited him even more. Suddenly he turned out of the street. He went into a little dark alley behind the animal sheds.

For half an hour he stayed in the alley, smelling the strong odor of the pigs and cows. He let his mind play with the strange new thoughts that came to him. Carefully, he began to move farther down the alley. A dog came at him, and George drove it away with stones. Then a man appeared at the door of one of the houses and yelled at the dog. George went into an empty lot. He threw back his head and looked up at the sky. He felt like saying words without meaning.

*"Death,"* he muttered, *"night—the sea—
fear—loveliness."*

George Willard came out of the lot.
Again he stood on the sidewalk facing the
houses. He felt that somehow all the
people in the little street must be
brothers and sisters to him. He wished
he could call them out of their houses and
shake their hands.

"If only there were a woman here, I
would take hold of her hand. We would
run and run until we were both tired
out," he thought. "That would make me
feel better."

With the thought of a woman in mind,
George walked out of the street. He went
toward the house where Belle Carpenter
lived. He thought that she might
understand his mood. Always before, it
had seemed to him that Belle was using
him for some purpose. He had not
enjoyed the feeling. Now he thought that
he had become too big to be used.

When George got to Belle Carpenter's
house, there had already been a visitor

there before him. Ed Handby had come to the door. He had called Belle out of the house and tried to talk to her. He had meant to ask the woman to come away with him and to be his wife. But when she came to the door, he lost his nerve. That made him angry. "You stay away from that kid," he growled, thinking of George Willard. Beyond that, he didn't know what else to say, so he turned to go away.

"If I catch you together I'll break your bones and his too," he had said as he walked off. He didn't know why he had talked that way. The bartender had come to talk of love, not to threaten. He was angry with himself for what he had said.

When Ed Handby had gone, Belle went inside. She ran quickly upstairs. From a window, she watched him cross the street and sit down on a tree stump. In the dim light, the man sat still, holding his head in his hands. The sight of it made her happy. When George Willard came to the door, she greeted him with great feeling.

Then she quickly put on her hat. She thought that Ed Handby would follow, as she walked through the streets with young Willard. She wanted to make the bartender suffer.

For an hour Belle Carpenter and the young reporter walked under the trees in the sweet night air. George Willard was full of big words that night. The sense of power that had come to him in the alley stayed with him. He talked boldly, swinging his arms about.

More than anything, he wanted to make Belle Carpenter see that he had changed. "You'll find me different," he declared, looking into her eyes. "I don't know why, but it is so. You've got to see me as a man now. That's how it is."

Up and down the quiet moonlit streets went the woman and the boy. When George ran out of words, they turned down a side street. They went across a bridge and onto a path that ran up the side of a hill. The hill climbed up to the Winesburg Fair Grounds. Thick bushes and small trees grew on the hillside. The grassy open spaces were now stiff and frozen.

George Willard was happy that Belle had come with him to this place. He felt like a man. He had noticed that she had not seemed to be listening to his words. But the fact that she had come with him at all seemed to be enough. "Everything is different," he thought. Then he took hold of her shoulder and turned her about. As he stood looking at her, his eyes were bright with pride.

Belle Carpenter did not pull away. When he kissed her, she leaned against him and looked over his shoulder into the darkness. It seemed like she was waiting for something. Again George Willard's mind ran off into words. He had the same feeling that he had had in the alley. Holding the woman tightly, he whispered into the still night. *"Love,"* he whispered. *"Love and night and women."*

George Willard did not understand what happened to him that night on the hillside. Later, when he got to his own room, he wanted to cry. Then he grew crazy with anger and hate. He hated Belle Carpenter and was sure that all his life he would continue to hate her. What had happened on the hill had broken his heart. He had led the woman to one of the little open spaces among the bushes. He had dropped to his knees beside her, feeling the new power in himself. He was waiting for Belle to speak when Ed Handby appeared.

The bartender did not want to beat the boy. Even if George had tried to take his woman away, Handby knew he did not need to use his fists. He grabbed George by the shoulder and pulled him to his feet. He held onto him with one hand as he looked at Belle Carpenter seated on the grass. Then, with a quick wide move of his arm, he threw George aside. His gesture sent the younger man flying away into the bushes. Handby began to shout at the woman who had risen to her feet. "You're no good!" he said. "I've half a mind not to bother with you. I'd let you alone—if I didn't care for you so much."

On his hands and knees in the bushes, George Willard could scarcely think. He got ready to spring at the man who had embarrassed him. To be beaten seemed far more manly than to be simply tossed aside.

Three times the young reporter sprang at Ed Handby. Each time the bartender caught him by the shoulder and tossed him back into the bushes. The older man seemed ready to repeat this exercise forever. But then George Willard's head hit the root of a tree and he lay still. Ed Handby took Belle Carpenter by the arm and marched her away.

George heard the man and woman making their way through the bushes. As he crept down the hillside, his heart felt sick. He hated himself. He hated the world. When his mind went back to the hour he had spent in the alley, he was confused. He stopped in the dark and listened. He hoped to hear again the voice outside himself. So short a time before, that voice had filled him with new courage. But now there was only silence.

His way home led him again through the street of frame houses. Now he could not bear the sight. He began to run. He wanted to get quickly out of the neighborhood that now seemed to him so very shabby and ordinary.

# Thinking About the Stories

## Sophistication

1. All stories fit into one or more categories. Is this story serious or funny? Would you call it an adventure, a love story, or a mystery? Is it a character study? Or is it simply a picture the author has painted of a certain time and place? Explain your thinking.

2. Story ideas come from many sources. Do you think this story is drawn more from the author's imagination or from real-life experience? What clues in "About the Author" might support your opinion?

3. Suppose this story had a completely different outcome. Can you think of another effective ending for this story?

The Untold Lie

1. Who is the main character in this story? Who are one or two of the minor characters? Describe each of these characters in one or two sentences.

2. What is the title of this story? Can you think of another good title?

3. Good writing always has an effect on the reader. How did you feel when you finished reading this story? Were you surprised, horrified, amused, sad, touched, or inspired? What elements in the story made you feel that way?

Paper Pills

1. Look back at the illustration that introduces this story. What character or characters are pictured? What is happening in the scene? What clues does the picture give you about the time and place of the story?

2. Some stories are packed with action. In other stories, the key events take place in the minds of the characters. Is this story told more through the characters' thoughts and feelings? Or is it told more through their outward actions?

3. All the events in a story are arranged in a certain order, or sequence. Tell about one event from the beginning of this story, one from the middle, and one from the end. How are these events related?

An Awakening

1. The plot is the series of events that takes place in a story. Usually, story events are linked in some way. Can you name an event in this story that was the cause of a later event?

2. Story ideas come from many sources. Do you think this story is drawn more from the author's imagination or from real-life experience? What clues in "About the Author" might support your opinion?

3. Imagine that you have been asked to write a short review of this story. In one or two sentences, tell what the story is about and why someone would enjoy reading it.

# Thinking About
# the Book

1. Choose your favorite illustration in this book. Use this picture as a springboard to write a new story. Give the characters different names. Begin your story with something they are saying or thinking.

2. Compare the stories in this book. Which was the most interesting? Why? In what ways were they alike? In what ways different?

3. Good writers usually write about what they know best. If you wrote a story, what kind of characters would you create? What would be the setting?

# LAKE CLASSICS

### Great American Short Stories I

Washington Irving, Nathaniel Hawthorne, Mark Twain, Bret Harte, Edgar Allan Poe, Kate Chopin, Willa Cather, Sarah Orne Jewett, Sherwood Anderson, Charles W. Chesnutt

### Great American Short Stories II

Herman Melville, Stephen Crane, Ambrose Bierce, Jack London, Edith Wharton, Charlotte Perkins Gilman, Frank R. Stockton, Hamlin Garland, O. Henry, Richard Harding Davis

### Great British and Irish Short Stories

Arthur Conan Doyle, Saki (H. H. Munro), Rudyard Kipling, Katherine Mansfield, Thomas Hardy, E. M. Forster, Robert Louis Stevenson, H. G. Wells, John Galsworthy, James Joyce

### Great Short Stories from Around the World

Guy de Maupassant, Anton Chekhov, Leo Tolstoy, Selma Lagerlöf, Alphonse Daudet, Mori Ogwai, Leopoldo Alas, Rabindranath Tagore, Fyodor Dostoevsky, Honoré de Balzac

Cover and Text Designer: Diann Abbott

Library of Congress Catalog Number: 94-075020
ISBN 1-56103-010-4
Printed in the United States of America
1 9 8 7 6 5 4 3 2 1

## LAKE CLASSICS

*Great American
Short Stories I*

# Sherwood
# ANDERSON

Stories retold by Joanne Suter
Illustrated by James Balkovek

**LAKE EDUCATION**
Belmont, California